Tantric Loving

Sacred Sexuality for Singles and Couples

Catherine Auman, LMFT

Green Tara Press

© 2025 Catherine Auman

Green Tara Press
Los Angeles, CA

www.greentarapress.com

Author cover photo by Charity Burnett
Author interior photo by Stephanie Westfall
Cover image by Anna Heimkreiter
Cover and interior book design by Lilly Penhall

"The Disciplines of Pleasure" and "You Can Induce Bliss at any Moment" were previously published in Catherine Auman's book *Shortcuts to Mindfulness: 100 Ways to Personal and Spiritual Growth.*

All Rights Reserved.

>Auman, Catherine I.

>Tantric Loving: Sacred Sexuality for Singles and Couples

>Self-Help 2. Relationships 3. Spiritual

Tradepaper ISBN: 978-1-945085-52-9

Ebook ISBN: 978-1-945085-53-6

Praise for Catherine Auman

"Oh my gosh, that book was so good! It is the best relationship book I have read in a long time. I reviewed it and purchased the other two in the series! Thank you so much for sharing your wisdom with the world!"

Marie Thouin, PhD, author of *What is Compersion: Understanding Positive Empathy in Consensually Non-Monogamous Relationships*

"The author is the real deal and she teaches that love is always available and changing our perception is an important place to begin."

Corey Lyon Folsom, author of *Soul Statements: A Love Coach's Guide to Successful Communication*

"Every little chapter is an energy hit for people, period, no matter what your level of experience. Easy to read pithy bites will raise your day to new heights."

Ginny Winn, LMFT, author of *Grievous Angels, Trout Masks, and American Beauties: 1970s Rock & Roll Photography*

"Full of insights and perspectives that will benefit any relationship and your life in general. The book is enjoyable to read and will deepen all your relationships."

Shanti Grace, Chief Administrative Officer, Brain Research Institute, UCLA (retired)

"I highly recommend Catherine's book to anyone looking for a new strategy on how to have more positive relationships with people, whether that is in the dating world or anywhere else."

Nicole Slater, Strategic Marketing and Personal Development Consultant

CONTENTS

Introduction 7

TANTRIC LOVING MINDSET

Sex is Sacred, Sometimes........................ 13
Tantric Sex vs. Conventional Sex 17
What? Are You Kidding? Why Would I Not
Want to Come?................................. 21
Becoming a Tantric Lover 25
Sexual Mindfulness, or Right Here, Right Now..... 29
Hungry for Touch.............................. 33
Conscious Touch is the Foundation of all
Tantric Sex.................................... 35
Making Love the Tantric Way.................... 39
Three Types of Orgasm (for Her)................. 43
Two Types of Orgasm (for Him) 47
Full-Body Orgasms (for Everyone) 51
Weird Pretzel Positions 55
When Your Mind is Running the Show 57
Relaxation is the Key 61
Never Stop Making Love........................ 63

TANTRIC LOVING EXERCISES

Exercise #1: The Disciplines of Pleasure 67
Exercise #2: You Can Induce Bliss at any Moment . . 71
Exercise #3: Practicing Conscious Touch 75
Exercise #4: Conscious Lovemaking:
Set and Setting 79
Exercise #5: The Valley Orgasm 81
Exercise #6: Tantric Embodiment Induction 83

About the Author 91
Connect with Catherine Auman 93
Tantric Mastery Series 95
Works by Catherine Auman 97

INTRODUCTION

I always wanted to be good in bed. (Doesn't everybody?) In my journey to become so, I read scads of books, perused online articles, checked out videos including porn . . . whatever seemed like it might help. I taught myself to have clitoral orgasms from instruction in a book, and expanded that into being able to have them on my back as it seemed it would be more convenient that way with a partner. Once I secretly bought a DVD about how to give killer blowjobs. I visited sex shops to see what I might learn there while considering the whips, chains, purple and animal-print dildos, and stripper outfits.

It was difficult to figure out how to be a sexy girl when I wasn't one of the ones with a perfect body or giant blown-up bubble breasts. I felt foolish wearing costumes; my boyfriend didn't care one whit about my garter belt; and I wasn't turned on by tying or being tied up. Even though I mastered a few skills that seemed to delight my partners, the whole process of producing an orgasm or two on cue was surprisingly lonely, and didn't seem to be the point. What else was there? Why did I have such a strong urge to understand sex, when everything I was doing kept turning out to be so unsatisfying?

For a while I hung out on the fringes of a group that identified itself as sex positive. They sponsored events and scripted encounters in all kinds of configurations: couples, three-ways, groups; with oil and without. I liked some of these people's intelligence, the fact that they lived outside the mainstream and were sexually uninhibited, but I didn't want to participate in their gatherings. I was always craving my own partner, just me and him. That became a lifetime spiritual search, outlined in my other books. My quest for sex to become what I dreamed it could be became the impetus for this book.

Then for a year I lived in the tantra ashram in India. I know that sounds like it must have been one long orgy, but the teachings we were involved in weren't about sex per se. Instead, we learned about tantra as a method of self-development, a way of releasing our wounding around sexuality, and dealing with our fears and resentments of the same and opposite genders. One of the reasons tantric sex is reputedly better than conventional sex is because it is engaged in by people who have made progress on their personal and spiritual growth paths. We were learning how to become tantric lovers, and that's what I want to share with you.

I was originally going to title this book *Tantric Lovemaking*. It's the fourth book in *The Tantric Mastery Series—Tantric Dating, Tantric Mating*, and *Tantric Relating*—but I've had some trouble with Amazon banning my books because they think they're pornography. If you've read them, you know they're about relationships and becoming a more loving person, and to think they're pornographic is a colossal misunderstanding. This book is about the sacredness of sex, so I'm happy to name it *Tantric Loving: Sacred Sexuality for Singles and Couples*. I hope you agree that's a beautiful concept.

The first book, *Tantric Dating* shares the secrets of why you haven't found love and how to find it. *Tantric Mating* illuminates how to be in partnership and create your perfect soulmate relationship. *Tantric Relating* is about how you can communicate both verbally and non- to keep the love fires burning, and to how to find and keep the sex, love and romance of your dreams. This book, *Tantric Loving* is about learning to honor yourself, your lover(s), and your lovemaking as sacred.

In this book, you'll learn how to make love in a way that is literally love-making, that is, it increases the sex, love, and romance in your life instead of causing pain and resentment for at least one of you. It's about overflowing with the goodness love creates, and being brought to tears by the overwhelming beauty of it all. How could we have ever allowed anyone to tell us that sex is sinful, when it is so obviously a gift from the divine? We stand for love; we stand for lovemaking, and for sharing love though sexual pleasure. When you make love the tantric way, there is no end to the possibilities for enduring, ecstatic love between you and your partner.

Because it's not really about big balloon boobs or oversized dicks; it's not about being skinny and young or even limber. It's not about peculiar positions or huffing and puffing. It's about you showing up as you—yes you, cellulite, spare tire, and all—and you being you as you are right now, willing to share exquisite time and connection with your special friend. That may not sound sexy, but hopefully by the end of this book, if I do my job right, you'll agree that that sounds like the hottest thing you've ever heard.

TANTRIC LOVING MINDSET

Sex is Sacred, Sometimes

The tantric view is that everything is sacred, all the time. There's no "sometimes" about it. However, most of us were raised with the belief that while some things are sacred, sex is not one of them. Basically, it was the patriarchal religions, Christianity, Judaism, and Islam, that taught that our bodies and sensual lives are not sacred—and, by the way, women are the cause of that.

Other worldviews exist, however, that predate these religions. It seems that long ago, there were people for whom the body, and in particular female bodies, were not denigrated, and sex was worshipped as sacred. If you Google the statues in Khajuraho, you'll find an ancient Indian culture that sculpted images on their temples of lovers engaged in sex acts. In Tibetan Buddhism, there are effigies and paintings of lovers sitting in *yab yum*, a lovemaking position that brings the two hearts together. I invite you to compare these attitudes with our modern-day culture which would consider such images pornographic.

In today's world, we are constantly being exposed to images of people having sex in ways that are exploitative, violent, uncaring, or just plain selfish. This seeps into our consciousness, and may be an influence if you're finding that the sex you're having is further and further away from what you've dreamed of. Perhaps if we begin to consider sex as sacred, these media portrayals of sexuality will not seem attractive to us anymore.

Instead, if you learn to make love in the tantric way, you'll begin to honor your own body as well as your partner's, create a sacred space to make love in, bring the sex energy into your heart, and practice sexual mindfulness. When tantrikas make love, we honor our partner's divinity, our own divinity, and the sacredness of the sexual connection between us.

Maybe you've been with a lover where, for a moment, you've been in an altered state of consciousness and felt the divine presence, or, something greater than the two of you. If you've had such an exceptional experience, you felt yourself to be in touch with the sacred. It can be a stretch to learn to see the divine in your lover's eyes, or to experience sensual pleasure as a gift from god, but that's what tantra is inviting you to do.

Would you like sex to be sacred in your life? It will take some work to reject the cultural brainwashing that teaches that there's something wrong with sex, and something wrong with you for coming out of the closet and saying, "Yes! I like sex, and I'm not ashamed to say it." Perhaps sex is one of the languages god speaks through.

Tantric Sex vs. Conventional Sex

Tantric sex is as great as they say it is, but not in the way most people think. It's not about better, faster, harder, more exotic conventional sex—It's actually a completely different approach to lovemaking.

Conventional sex is about performing a script we've been taught. We've been brainwashed to believe that sex follows a certain linear formula that consists of foreplay, she comes, he comes, and it's over. While that is better than in the olden days when nobody cared if she enjoyed it, it's still a strict procedure we've been taught to follow and never question. What if that weren't the only way or even the best way to have sex?

Conventional sex has taught us that orgasm is the prize we're going for. All of our actions are leading to that big payoff. Every touch and every stroke are secretly evaluated as to whether they are getting us closer to the big bang or leading us away. This kind of sex leads to a lot of frustration because you might feel that your partner is not "doing it right" for you to get off.

Tantric sex is very different from all that. First of all, tantric lovers are not going for the goal of orgasm. Secondly, we don't think young, thin bodies are more attractive than older or bigger ones. We are fascinated by real people and relish the variety: the soft body, the freckled, the out-of-shape. Third, we don't go along with the whole having-sex-according-to-script thing either. We like to mix it up, maybe do this for a while, then that.

So what are tantric lovers doing then? Mindfully staying in the present moment and exploring what happens with this partner—does this stroke excite them? Do we feel closer and more in love when I touch this way? When we gaze into each other's eyes do we feel a connection with the Universe? What happens when we don't come? Tantric lovers are more interested in how connected we are with our partner, how intimate. The intention is to relate so closely that magic happens. The purpose is not to act like porn stars, but to be our most vulnerable intimate self, and to bring that to lovemaking. Then we can be so close we actually "make(more) love."

CONVENTIONAL SEX	TANTRIC SEX
Goal Oriented	Goal-Less
Orgasm Focused	Orgasmic Waves
Is Over Quickly	Often Lasts for Hours
Goes Downhill With Time	Always New
Naughty	Sacred
Coming is in the Future	The Present Moment
Right and Wrong Ways To Do It	Connection
Declines With Age	Only Gets Better
Mostly Seen as Separate from Love	Sex = Love

What? Are You Kidding? Why Would I Not Want to Come?

The simple answer is that coming stops things; and if the lovemaking is delicious, why would you want to stop? The full answer goes much deeper, however, and some of the following might make you feel like your head is going to explode. That's how I felt, at least, when I started grokking the magnitude of this thing.

First of all, we've been taught that sex is one thing and one thing only, that is, both people getting to their orgasm as quickly and efficiently as possible. But that's not the way most women (and many men) enjoy making love. In studies, women have shown that they prefer affectionate touch, romance, and a quality relationship over strictly genital contact. As many as 50% of women do not orgasm on demand as science has decided they should, and are thus considered "dysfunctional."

What if orgasm isn't the point? It's only been since the 1920s that sexological scientists have proclaimed it so. In the 1960s Masters & Johnson codified a kind of linear sex that headed straight for the conclusion of orgasm for both parties, and that was deemed the way it should be for everyone. Turns out that that research was flawed, but the damage has been done to millions who have been taught that how they preferred to make love was not "how it's supposed to be." What if everything you've been taught about sex is wrong? That's what nearly burst my head open, just considering that possibility.

When you make love without the goal of orgasm (or ejaculation), every touch is different than it used to be. When you aren't touching with the goal of getting your partner to their point of no-return, you can luxuriate in the joy of the moment, exploring their skin and their response, and getting lost in your own ecstasy. When instead you've been focused on getting them and yourself off, you're concerned with whether what you or they are doing is "right." In tantra, there is no right way.

This really can't be understood by reading about it, so I hope you will try it out with a partner. If you don't have a partner, you can experiment with yourself. What happens if you self-pleasure with the intent to quickly orgasm and get on with it (nothing wrong with that—it's just limited) vs. self-pleasuring for a period of time just to make love to yourself? Also, there is quite a bit of evidence that orgasming saps your energy that you might need for other things. See if that's true for you.

It's not that tantrikas never orgasm, ejaculate, or have hot, heavy sex. Of course we do. We've just learned that making love the tantric way offers unheard of delights that you can only access if you aren't focused on getting to the Big O.

Becoming a Tantric Lover

Becoming a tantric lover is a commitment, a joy, a responsibility, and potentially a lifelong journey. One of the best things about the tantric path is that you don't have to do anything. Unlike in the conventional sex world, you aren't considered better if you're gorgeous, highly Botox'ed, or possess pornstar sexual skills. (Nothing's wrong if you are those things either; tantra's about you being you.) All that's gently recommended is that you become more mindful about being in your own body and in being present with the body of another person.

So beginning with that, to develop as a tantric lover, **engage in some sort of mindfulness practice.** This could be one of the many formal methods of sitting in meditation, such as zazen, Transcendental Meditation, or a yoga practice. It could be simple reminders on Post-its that you review several times a day to wake yourself up and be aware of your body. As your awareness begins to more and more permeate the geography below your neck, the better lover you will become.

Tantra is a lot about **healing yourself:** our wounded bodies, emotions, and sexuality. Many of you can benefit from psychotherapy to recover from childhood trauma, past relationships, and growing up in a sex-negative culture where sex is not considered sacred or loving. There are also a lot of great self-help books and videos available to help you on your healing journey.

Tantric lovers come in all shapes and sizes. I've met tantrikas with bodies that are quadriplegic, XXX-large, in their 70s, ones who possess an impressive amount of cellulite, had a breast removed due to cancer, or are the owners of extra-small penises or lop-sided boobs. It's great if you're able to **keep your body healthy** by exercising, but even if you can't, you can always eat better and breathe more deeply. (Or maybe you can't. If you can, give thanks.)

Some people think they'll **commit to love** when they find the right person, but the truth is, you'll never find the right person until you commit to love. Love is not about fulfilling a fantasy. It's about becoming a lover, literally, a person who loves.

Commit to the Path of Love. **The path of the tantric lover is the path of love.**

Sexual Mindfulness: Right Here, Right Now

If you've practiced mindfulness meditation, you know that it involves slowing way down, paying attention to your breath, being aware of your physical sensations, of your body in this moment, of sitting here in this chair. It involves being aware of what's going on inside your body, of kinesthetic experiences such as smells and sounds, and of being present. Mindfulness is ignoring or not paying attention to what's going on in your mind. The mind, as you know, is constantly churning, imagining exciting things, criticizing you, recalling the past and imagining the future, thinking about what's for lunch; in short, thinking about everything except what's really happening in the present, right here, right now. In some mindfulness practices, they call this "the monkey mind" because it never stops chattering.

In mindfulness, you let all that stuff go. You're just noticing what's actually here. When you bring this state of awareness to a sexual situation, it's called sexual mindfulness. In your own presence and/or in the presence of a partner, you drop the thinking and bring your awareness to what's actually happening right now. Maybe you are caressing your own arm or the arm of a beloved. Perhaps you notice the rise and fall of your own breath or that of your lover's, or you focus on that soft meditative music you've put on to enhance your experience. Maybe you notice a warm feeling inside your tummy. There's no hurry, no need to get anywhere, just a chance to savor the preciousness of what's happening in the present moment.

Several scientific studies have been conducted in the last ten years that show that people who practice mindfulness in a sexual encounter report better self-esteem, more satisfaction with their partner, and greater happiness with their sex lives. Who wouldn't want that? Those are all great outcomes, and it turns out that sexual mindfulness is the gateway to expanded states of consciousness, conscious touch, and tantric loving.

When you're looking to start cultivating tantric loving, the first step is to practice mindfulness any time, including when you're in the bedroom. It means being present with your lover without focusing on the future, without paying attention to "am I doing it right?" and not rushing toward orgasm. It means not judging yourself or your partner, but letting it be—letting performance anxiety go and just being present with what is. This is what spiritual teachers talk about: being present in this moment. You bring this meditative quality to your sex life, and your sex life becomes part of your spiritual path.

Hungry for Touch

Virginia Satir, one of the inventors of family therapy, was quoted as saying, "We need 4 hugs a day for survival. We need 8 hugs a day for maintenance. We need twelve hugs a day for growth." I certainly don't get that many a day, do you? Touch has been proven in studies to be essential for well-being, and it can improve mood, boost your immune system, reduce stress and anxiety, and strengthen your bonds with others. Since most of us never get the hugs we need on a daily basis, we suffer from what I call "skin hunger."

I noticed this when I was living at the tantra ashram in India. On the Main Road I would notice mothers dressed in colorful saris with their children hanging all over them, one holding her hand, another hanging across her chest, and another grasping her leg. Men friends would walk hand in hand without worrying that this might mean they were lovers. Everywhere people were touching, holding, and being physically close. It looked so different from our western world.

Not only have you not been touched enough, your lover hasn't either. This is one reason in tantra we make love for such long periods of time. It feels so reparative to be stroked lovingly, to be held—not for any reason, not so the other person can "get off," but merely two humans who care about each other exchanging affection in a luxurious, all-the-time-in-the-world fashion. Your partner may appear quite self-contained and not touch-starved, but if they come from this culture, you can be sure that there is a touch deficit.

Not only have our bodies not been sufficiently embraced, but sexually our genitals have not been touched enough. When we use each other only for getting off and having an orgasm, these needs for touch only intensify rather than heal. Check in with yourself: Have you and your partner shared enough cuddling? Enjoyed enough oral sex? Make a vow to make up for lost time.

When you practice tantric lovemaking, you want to make sure you and your lover receive enough touch. This is another reason we don't think getting to orgasm quickly is the point of sex. What if it isn't orgasm we are hungry for, but rather the sweet, nurturing, long-lasting caress of our lover, our friend?

Conscious Touch is the Foundation of all Tantric Sex

Conscious touch means bringing the mindfulness you've been practicing into whenever you touch someone's body or when you're being touched, rather than doing it unconsciously. What you're going for is to get your attention onto the point where your bodies are contacting each other and then attempting to keep it there. When the mind starts thinking, as it always does, you gently bring your attention back to your body and the point where it is touching or being touched by your partner.

You can practice this on yourself, and you can practice on your lover. When I was single, I wanted to build my ability to remain conscious while I was touching and being touched, so I went for a massage once a week. As a meditation, I would keep my attention on where the massage therapist was touching me, on the point of contact between our bodies. This skill helps with lovemaking because you want to be able to stay in your awareness and not be thinking about lunch.

Conventional sexual touch has the purpose of increasing arousal. You touch your partner with the intention to heighten their turn-on, to get them ready for the ensuing big bang of orgasm. In conscious touch and therefore in tantra, that's not the purpose. The only purpose is to be fully present and to share love.

So, to practice conscious touch:

- **Be in your body, not your head**
  Stop thinking! Or watch your thoughts happening, but don't pay attention to them.

- **Go with whatever arises**
  Maybe your arousal is lessening—is that necessarily a bad thing? Maybe you want to take a break and cuddle, or talk about something. Maybe you're releasing some old sexual trauma, and just want your partner to hold you. It's all good.

- **Enjoy prolonged pleasuring**
 What if pleasure and connecting with your partner were the point of lovemaking, rather than orgasm?

- **Focus awareness inside your own body, or inside the place where your partner is touching**
 What's it like to keep your awareness inside your body? Go inside and take a look around.

- **Focus on what you like, not what you don't**
 If you focus on what you don't like, you'll feel frustrated, and your mind will ruin your experience. Instead, pay attention to what your partner is doing that you like.

- **Expanding to enjoy this**
 Ask yourself if you can expand to enjoy what is happening even more!

- **Attention on the point of contact**
 Keep your attention on the point where your skin and your partner's skin are touching—the point of contact.

Making Love the Tantric Way

Now that you've prepared yourself by practicing mindfulness, keeping your body healthy, healing yourself, committing to love, and conscious touch, how do tantric lovers make love?

Tantric lovers don't focus on orgasm. If orgasms happen, they happen, but it's not the end goal as it is in conventional sex. What is the goal then, if there is one? Connection. Drinking in, drowning in, delighting in that special thing that happens when two people make love, that third thing that is given life, that is born. There are times when you go so deep you realize why it's called "making love"—because that is what you are literally doing with your bodies and souls—making more love between you two.

How do you make love the tantric way? You surrender to the body's lead. If you pay attention through sexual mindfulness, your body and your touch will lead you. You don't have to worry about getting to the next level of arousal, because where you are right now is perfect. Feel that, feel its perfection. Can you expand that awareness further inside yourself? Can you enjoy it more? In conventional sex, we're often trying to enjoy it more by pointing out to our partner how they're not pleasing us correctly. Focus on enjoying more what they are doing, because if you're not going for orgasm, there is no wrong touch (unless they're hurting you and you don't want to be hurt).

What happened for my husband and I was that making love this way turned us into people who knew how to do relationships. We both had painful relationship histories, so we were only looking for something quite not as bad as last time. Instead, the love we shared by making love tantrically and not focusing on orgasm created so much love that we automatically treated each other with respect. There were no power struggles, no sniping, no "teasing" that isn't really teasing—it all went away in the ocean of cosmic vibrations that you are floating in when you are not performing sex in order to get to orgasm. When you stop performing, you get to really BEING; then it's two souls making love through their bodies instead of two egos using their bodies to get off

You enter into lovemaking with the most open willingness to be surprised, with a surrender to the higher consciousness that will bless you through its presence. Your only job is to be present and to let yourself relax and enjoy.

3 Types of Orgasm (for Her)

We've talked quite a bit now about how tantric sex is not about orgasm, mostly that is, not striving toward producing an orgasm. However, orgasms will happen when you truly surrender, and these orgasms are of a different caliber than what you may be used to. I like to call them orgasmic waves rather than orgasms, because you might miss them if you're used to the big bang orgasms that come from strictly clitoral stimulation.

What if orgasm isn't about "doing?" Only one kind of orgasm is about doing, and that is the clitoral orgasm. The clitoris likes a lot of direct stimulation—rubbing, licking, stroking, teasing—by a partner, a sex toy, or by yourself. This kind of orgasm is similar to men's orgasms that come with ejaculation—you feel yourself getting close, so you tense your muscles and deepen your breath and make it happen. Then after one or three of them, you feel finished and done with sex.

The G-spot and the cervix are located inside the vagina. When they are stroked lovingly and mindfully, orgasms may occur which have less to do with "doing." Internal orgasms such as these can go on and on, indefinitely, as long as the stimulation is present. They are not the result of building up tension in order to release it and feel different from those produced by clitoral stimulation. Clitoral orgasms purposely build tension to a higher and higher peak until they feel like they explode. On the other hand, women often don't know when they're having vaginal orgasms because they're not intense in the same way that clitoral orgasms are. They're more like rippling waves, and they take you over, and it seems that the amount of time they can last perhaps is infinite, or at least until you get tired. The waves take you over and rock you. With this kind of orgasm, you don't want to stop; you want to keep making love.

These internal female orgasms don't require effort at all. They just happen if you're relaxed and present enough. That might take some practice—to be mindful enough while making love and to choose the right partner with whom you can be truly relaxed. That might take some work on your relationship. That might take getting to be comfortable in your own body in the presence of your lover.

These three types of orgasms come naturally to some, but not most, women. Others may need to heal their G-spots and cervixes from trauma, a topic we will cover in a later book. For now, it's important to know that if you are not orgasming vaginally, there's nothing wrong with you, it's merely a step on your ongoing journey of personal and spiritual growth. It's ahead of you, and it's something to look forward to.

Two Types of Orgasm (for Him), or, Orgasm vs. Ejaculation

Conventional sex teaches that for men, orgasm and ejaculation are the same thing. It's rarely even questioned whether a man's coming is the point, because, after all, his ejaculation means sex is over. Actually, if you pay attention closely and mindfully, you'll observe that orgasm in men happens moments before the ejaculation does. It's possible for men to orgasm, even have a full-body orgasm, and not ejaculate.

Since we've been taught that male orgasm and ejaculation are the same thing, many men, by frequent pornography use, are training their bodies that sex is about intensifying their energy up, up, up until ejaculation is the prize, and then it's over. Porn includes nothing at all about the emotional, relational, or loving aspects of sex, and when this stimulation to ejaculation is repeated over and over, it can encourage men to prioritize coming over caring.

Other cultures have understood that ejaculation is not the ultimate point of sex, unless of course, you're trying to create a baby. In the ancient Chinese and contemporary Taoist sexual arts, they believe that it's unhealthy for men to ejaculate frequently. This is controversial, but if you're going to enjoy long, extended periods of tantric lovemaking, the man doesn't want to ejaculate because, well, then it's over. If you prefer to have conventional sex, fine, it's all good. But if you want to learn tantric lovemaking where you can make love for hours and hours without Viagra or Cialis, it takes the man learning to relax and control his ejaculation.

There are many techniques in the Taoist erotic arts to stop ejaculation. What we've found is that it's already too late at that point. Instead, what you want to do is when you are nearing the point of orgasm, is you relax instead. That's it. Rather than increasing the intensity to get up to these high levels of arousal where you're about to explode, you relax, surrendering to the blissful sexual energy without having to get anywhere else, that is, orgasm. You focus on the sensations in your whole body, not just your genitals. You stay hard and experience orgasmic waves instead of ejaculating and being forced to stop.

Besides when the man ejaculates, it's over, and if the sex is really good, who wants to stop? An untold number of the sexual partners of men are laying there at night trying to sleep, frustrated that the sexual encounter was far too short. If you never try non-ejaculatory sex, you'll never have the opportunity to see if it works for you. Men are capable of multiple orgasms, very similar to the ones women experience with the rippling effect of orgasmic waves. They can just go on and on . . .

Full-Body Orgasm (for Everyone)

In our sex-negative culture, it's no surprise that we've learned to be uncomfortable with sexual feelings in our bodies. We've been brainwashed that we must only be attracted to the "right" people, and that there's something wrong with us if we're attracted to people who are not the cultural ideal of the moment. We've been taught that when we're with a lover and we have sexual arousal in our bodies, we must get rid of it (discharge) the energy as quickly as possible in an orgasm. We go on repeating this quick arousal-and-discharge pattern and wonder why our sex lives are so unsatisfying.

In tantra, we work with our body and emotions until we don't feel uncomfortable with sexual charge in our bodies, in fact, we enjoy it immensely. We can walk around all day with a turn-on in any kind of environment and not feel like we have to get rid of it or do anything about it. People are afraid of their sexual charge because they think they're going to have to act on it, such as pursue or flirt with the person they feel it with, and they don't particularly want to. In tantra, we just enjoy the arousal. You notice you're attracted to that person, and you're not going to do anything about it other than enjoy it. The other person doesn't even have to know. You're just going to enjoy the feeling of sexual turn-on in your body.

Once you create and expand this ability to tolerate increased levels of sexual pleasure instead of having to get rid of it, you are increasing your capacity for full body orgasms. You allow the sexual energy to expand beyond the genitals and into the whole body. You don't have to discharge the energy in a short period of time.

As you practice making love without having to get rid of the energy through orgasm, you can build the capacity to have full body orgasms wherein the whole body will vibrate, not just the genitals having their little spasm. It's a beautiful thing to develop this capacity in yourself, and practicing being in the present moment will help.

Most of us have heard about the possibility of full body orgasms for women, but maybe not so much the possibility of full body orgasms for men, but full body orgasms are available for everybody.

They don't just happen though, usually. More likely, there's a sense of developing ourselves as lovers before this is possible. So you want to get into your body, get your consciousness into your body, practice conscious touch, have some kind of body discipline. You pay attention, you are mindful, you have cultivated your mind to be able to be silent at least some of the time, and you know you're a work in progress.

Weird Pretzel Positions

Many people think that tantra means making love in weird pretzel positions, such as hanging from the ceiling, or twisting and turning in ways that you'd have to be really agile to perform. None of that is necessary. Any position can be full of unknown delight, if you experience it through new eyes, ears, and touch.

Kenneth Ray Stubbs, a tantra teacher, once told a story about writing a book on tantra that nobody bought. He changed the title to *Secret Sexual Positions,* and it began to sell. People seem to like the idea that there are secret postures out there that are going to do it for them, or will at least relieve the boredom of conventional sex. Go ahead and experiment with all the positions you want, but that's not what tantra is about.

In tantra we might find ourselves making love in the same position every time, and every time feels new. We're not focusing on novelty, because we're focusing our attention on what's new about this delight and pleasure. Perhaps we've never noticed how beautiful our lover's skin is, or paid attention to the exquisite thrill of their caress.

A famous Greek philosopher named Heraclites said, "You never step into the same river twice." The person you're making love with is not the same as they were yesterday, and you are not either. In tantra, you haven't made love with this partner today and they're not the same person as they were the last time you made love. It's totally new every time if you tune in to the newness of every moment.

Try this: Go ahead and practice any new sexual position you're attracted to. Have fun! Then try this: Make love in any-old familiar position, and notice what's new about it. Pay attention to what you've never observed before: what do you see, hear, smell, touch, taste? Have you ever noticed that mole on their back? That blush that spreads over their chest? What's never captured your attention before? What's beautiful and precious, vulnerable and sweet about your partner? How about what's strong and admirable? You see, if you're bored in sex (or in life for that matter), it only means you're not paying attention.

When Your Mind is Running the Show

If you've ever meditated, you've undoubtedly noticed that your mind is a chatterbox. That's its nature, and during a mindfulness practice, your job is to watch the thoughts and not get lost in them. This is not particularly easy, and for many people, it takes years of discipline. When practicing sexual mindfulness, you may notice that the thoughts in your head are prattling on and on during lovemaking, and when they are, you can't be fully relaxed and present.

For example, you might be enjoying some luscious conscious touch with your lover, and you notice that your mind starts saying:

- "I wish this would hurry up."
- "I don't like that touch"
- "What's for dinner tonight?"

- "Is this thing I'm doing getting my partner off?"
- "Last time was better."
- "I'm bored."

All these thoughts are interfering with you being able to be loving in a tantric way with your partner. You might say to your mind:

- "I don't want to think about that right now. I want to be present."
- "That's just a thought. I'm not going to listen to my chattering mind."
- "Be silent and tune into the feelings instead of the thoughts."

And you orient your attention back to the point of contact between your bodies.

I heard once that the mind is great to have in the car, but it shouldn't be driving. Its rightful place is sitting in the backseat. You want to be the driver of your car, not your mind.

If your desire is to become a tantric lover, you'll want to cultivate this capacity to let your mind fall silent. Osho said that meditators make the best lovers, and this is why. Practice noticing the mind trying to run the show next time you're making love, and let it calm down. All you have to do is not pay attention to it. It doesn't need to stop; you just need to not feed it. You don't want to start an internal war trying to make it stop because that makes it worse. You just want to say, "I don't have to think about that right now." When your mind is running the show, you can't receive the great benefits of lovemaking. When you let the thoughts go, you invite the blessed silence.

Relaxation is the Key

The kind of sex we're taught to have in the conventional world is the opposite of relaxation. It's about creating tension in order to release tension. (Think about that for a minute—doesn't that seem a bit weird?) It's about ramping up the intensity and speed, putting your foot on the gas, and accelerating toward release. Sometimes this kind of sex is exhilarating and hot. At other times, having sex this way may feel like a conflict, a strain, a power struggle, or an anxiety. This can lead to suffering the mistrust these feelings engender, and people thinking there's something wrong with them.

In tantric lovemaking, we don't struggle to ramp it up. We watch the arousal arise on its own: The deliciousness of the turn-on is its own reward.

That doesn't mean that tantrikas don't have lusty, hot, erotic sex—we certainly do. The difference is that we're not struggling to rise up to those orgasmic levels, unless we want to. If we want to have a quickie, we're just the same as everybody else. If we want to create a short burst of sex, build up the tension, then let it go, then we'll do that too. There's nothing wrong with it—whatever kind of sex you enjoy is what you should be doing. Tantra is just letting you know there are options that you may not have heard of from mainstream sex pundits.

In tantric lovemaking, relaxation is the key. We are enjoying making love, not trying to get to the point where it ends. Relaxation is key for women to be able to surrender into those orgasmic waves, so this is why even conventional sex suggests that there be a certain period of time for "foreplay" before the "play" itself. For men, erections are the result of relaxation and of feeling comfortable with your partner. If the guy feels comfortable and trusts his partner, trusts the situation, he'll be able to get hard without any problem. It's when there's worry and lack of relaxation, lack of trusting this partner or the situation, that erectile dysfunction happens. This is contrary to regular advice, but it's the tantric way.

It may not be easy to relax in sex, especially when there's a lot of emotional unfinished business between you and your partner. This is why an ongoing practice of clearing (this concept is explained in detail in *Tantric Relating*) is essential for the highest and most loving tantric sex.

Never Stop Making Love

It's actually possible to never stop making love. Your whole life can be one long lovemaking. My husband Greg and I say that we never stop making love. We don't - we very rarely choose to orgasm so it rarely ends. It goes on and on, whether we're eating, working out at the gym, or visiting with friends. It may not be sexual lovemaking that includes intercourse, but it is us being together with great sexual chemistry that we keep stoked by the way we make love.

Someone once asked us in one of our workshops, "How do you know when to stop if you don't orgasm?" It's simple, really, you stop when you feel done. That might be in 15 minutes, or that might be in a couple hours. It might be when it's time to eat a snack or go to work. One of you might be tired or find that your mind is running the show so much you want to go do something else. It's all good. When you don't end with an orgasm, you just pick right up again the next time. There's no ending.

That way you're making love when you're eating together, watching Netflix, or cleaning the house.

Instead of saying, "Do you want to stop now?" you can say to your partner, "Shall we take a break?" That way you're just pausing for a period of time, knowing that you'll come back together. When you enter your sacred space to worship each other's bodies again, it never really stopped. The divine energy was just taking a break and you've been continuing to make love on another plane. Your whole life can be about making love.

If you never stop making love, you're always attracted to your partner. Attraction doesn't lessen or die as it does in conventional sex. When you're always aroused and haven't disbursed the energy, you won't have to get in the mood or get warmed up. You won't require a period of foreplay because you're already aroused.

You're doing your business, you're doing your work, you're doing all these other things that everyone else does, but always running in the background is the sense that you've not really stopped making love. You know you made love yesterday, you know you made love today, and you know you'll make love tomorrow. If you miss a day it doesn't matter, because you're still making love. It doesn't ever have to stop. It's a beautiful way to live. I urge you to try it.

TANTRIC LOVING EXERCISES

EXERCISE #1: THE DISCIPLINES OF PLEASURE

The word "discipline" is most often attached to things we don't want to do. We don't want to exercise and we don't want to eat right; therefore "discipline" seems like a bummer. Our idea of a well-disciplined person is close to that of a military recruit: rigid and tense, running his or her life like clockwork. It can seem that being well disciplined is saying a big "no" to life.

Hedonism, on the other hand, or the devotion to pleasure, is considered the opposite of discipline. We all pretty much agree on what is pleasurable: bad-for-you foods, beverages, and activities. As Mark Twain once said, "Too much whiskey is barely enough." The American way of hedonism is that if something is pleasurable, then more would be better.

Neither is true. One must discipline oneself in order to experience pleasure more frequently and more often. For example, you've probably figured out that you prefer drinking less alcohol than you did in college because you don't want the hangovers, which are decidedly un-fun. Drinking is certainly pleasurable; most people have decided it's more so in moderation. Delicious food is more pleasurable in small quantities, because then you can also enjoy the pleasure of a fit body rather than the anti-pleasures of obesity, diabetes, and heart disease. Many people who refuse discipline find themselves unable to experience pleasure due to sickness or malaise and enervation.

I was taught by one of my early tantra teachers that "pleasure requires constant vigilance." True hedonism requires discipline, because one must exercise mindful awareness of what will ultimately contribute to pleasure.

We can develop a practice of incorporating daily pleasurable experiences for the body. We're lucky in urban areas that massages, Jacuzzis, saunas, manicures and pedicures are affordable treats for women and men. We can practice looking at beauty in our many vistas of nature, or in the wonderful art museums (which all have free admission on certain days). We can hike in the hills, go for a swim, or exchange affection with a loved one. If we fail to discipline ourselves to take our pleasure seriously, we are prone to compulsively seek to fulfill this need through addictive pleasures. In other words, if we don't seek pleasure consciously, we will demand it in unconscious and unhealthy ways.

Many spiritual people try to deny their need for pleasure and deprive themselves, believing asceticism is the way to god. They think of the spiritual path as one of self-denial, fasting, weird restrictive diets, and forcing disciplines on themselves that they don't want and which may even be harmful. I would like to suggest that the spiritual path can be the most pleasurable of all—full of the disciplined pleasure of a great "yes" to life.

EXERCISE #2: YOU CAN INDUCE BLISS AT ANY MOMENT

People think that bliss states are dependent on buying and owning the right things, being in the right environment, finding a sexy partner, or years of spiritual discipline. The truth is, bliss states are available to you anytime, anywhere.

Such as right now. Walk with me through this technique I developed when I lived in India:

- **Unfocused Eyes** – As I've written before, the aggressive Western gaze reaches out and claims the environment, penetrating, owning, criticizing, and conquering. When we unfocus the eyes, they become soft and open to receive.

- **Be Breathed** – Slow your breathing down, all the way down. Notice the difference between when you are doing the breathing, such as when purposefully take a deep breath, and when the breathing is happening by itself. Are you breathing?

No, "something" or "someone" is breathing you. Enjoy being breathed: no effort is required.

- **All the Way to the Root** – In the modern world, we breathe rapidly and shallowly, with the breath staying at the top of the chest. If you look at statues of the Buddha, he has a big fat belly, symbolizing that his breath was so relaxed it went all the way into his abdomen. Bring the breath down to your tailbone. Let it push out your belly when it inhales, then deflate like a balloon during the exhale.

- **Watch the Flow** – Feel the breath flowing in and out by itself, over and over. Observe it circulating all the way down, up and out. If you are somewhere where there is activity, open to the flow of humanity or nature with your unfocused eyes. If your mind starts its endless judgment, watch that, too.

- **Blissfulness** – Become aware that blissfulness is happening. It may not be as dramatic as you have been led to believe, but there it is, flowing within you at all times, below the level of your awareness, just waiting for you to tune into its frequency. It's not anything you need to search for—it's been there all along.

This technique might be easiest to learn and practice lying silently in a quiet room, but you can practice on a busy city street, in a board meeting, or during an argument with your lover. These are more challenging situations, of course, but the point of any meditation practice is to bring these higher states into our daily lives.

EXERCISE #3: PRACTICING CONSCIOUS TOUCH

You may be already good at this, but it's a skill that you can always get better at. I'm still practicing daily.

Individually

Sit and quiet yourself. Run your fingers across your forearm. Take in the sensation, savor it. Feel it deeply in your fingertips. Go slower. See if you can enjoy it even more.

Without stopping your stroking, move your attention to inside your arm. Feel yourself being stroked. Deepen your awareness of receiving pleasure from the stroking.

Now alternate back and forth: first bringing attention to stroking, then to being stroked. Practice until you become a master of flipping your awareness to one, then the other.

When you feel as if you have the hang of this, drop your awareness into holding both at the same time: stroking and being stroked. Up your level of awareness, up your awareness of pleasure.

Flip back and forth between all three modes of awareness.

How could this enhance your lovemaking?

During Massage

This is an exercise I did weekly for at least a year before I was of an expanded-enough frequency to attract my Perfect Beloved.

I went to a place that offered Chinese Foot Massage (which is really a whole body massage, it's just called that). You can choose any kind of massage—it's just that this type is more affordable.

While receiving the massage, I would concentrate on keeping my awareness on the place where I was being touched, on the point of contact where the practitioner's hands were touching my body. This concentration increased my ability to be in-the-present and fully embodied, preparing me to be finely tuned for tantric lovemaking with my future partner.

I would also strive to be conscious of when my mind was being critical, often for no reason. If I had the thought, "This touch is too hard," I would ask myself if it was really too hard, or if I experienced it as too hard because I wasn't relaxed enough. It was almost always the latter. This helped me become more accepting of what is, and to get out of my own way and experience more pleasure.

EXERCISE #4: CONSCIOUS LOVEMAKING: SET AND SETTING

It is well-known in psychedelic circles that for an optimal experience when ingesting the sacred sacraments, you should consider set and setting. This means having the right mindset, such as being calm, relaxed, and open to new experience, and setting up a beautiful environment where you won't be disturbed and will feel safe. Here are some ideas for creating an optimal set and setting for tantric lovemaking:

Set:

1. Have you prepared yourself? Are you remembering your embodiment? Remembering to cherish the present moment instead of dwelling in "how it used to be" or fantasizing about the future? Making love is right now, in this body, with this special friend.
2. Have you and your partner cleared any issues that may be between you? Greg and I always sit for a while before making love

and discuss anything unspoken before we enter into our sacred space.
3. Are you both freshly bathed? Is this something you would like to do together? Do you enjoy perfume, or do you prefer the lovely scent of bare skin and sweat?

Setting:

4. Is your bedroom beautiful? Do you have freshly-washed sheets? Is there water handy? Have you thought about including little snacks in case lovemaking goes on for hours?
5. Make a playlist of trance-inducing music. Most "sexy" music is geared toward conventional sex that is headed toward orgasm. For starters, you can listen to my tantric lovemaking playlists on YouTube and Spotify, but as you go along, you will find your own music to enhance your and your partner's altered states.
6. Is there anything you might bring into your lovemaking space that would help you remember that you are sharing something sacred? Some people like spiritual artwork on the walls, candles, incense, crystals, statues, and special clothes.

EXERCISE #5: THE VALLEY ORGASM

"This is one type of orgasm—coming to the peak of excitement. Tantra is centered on another type of orgasm. If we call the first kind a peak orgasm, you can call the tantric orgasm a valley orgasm. In it you are not coming to the peak of excitement, but to the very deepest valley of relaxation. Excitement has to be used for both in the beginning. That is why I say that in the beginning both are the same, but the ends are totally different.

"Excitement has to be used for both: either you are going toward the peak of excitement or to the valley of relaxation. For the first, excitement has to be intense—more and more intense. You have to grow in it; you have to help it to grow towards the peak. In the second, excitement is just a beginning. And once the man has entered, both lover and beloved can relax. No movement is needed. They can relax in a loving embrace. When the man feels or the woman feels that the erection is going to be lost, only then is a little movement and excitement required. But then again relax. You can prolong this deep embrace for hours with no ejaculation, and then both can fall into deep sleep together. This—*this*—is a valley orgasm. Both are relaxed, and they meet as two relaxed beings."

– Osho, *The Book of Secrets*

1. When you read this quote, how does it make you feel? Is this something you would like to experience with your lover?
2. Regardless of your gender or the gender of your partner, how might the ideas in this quote apply to your own experiences or desires about lovemaking?

EXERCISE #6: TANTRIC EMBODIMENT INDUCTION

This is an exercise about coming into our bodies. It can be practiced over time to enhance your capacity as a tantric lover. You can read along and follow the prompts, or you can listen to an audio version by downloading it from my website at the QR code here:

Put your things down, and get into a comfortable position. This will be a little meditation—if you want to just sit, that's fine. If you do yoga, you might want to settle into a comfortable yoga posture. Nobody gets extra points for sitting stiffly and holding their breath. You get extra points for being really relaxed.

Listen, isn't that silence beautiful? If you want to you can close your eyes, or you can just lower them so you're not looking around. First, without trying to change anything, notice how you're breathing. The contemporary conventional culture keeps us breathing very shallowly and very rapidly. Just notice that. There's nothing wrong with it. We need to breathe that way to not take in everything, the traffic, everything that's so difficult. Just notice it. Now take a deep breath. Pretty much everyone knows that to take a deep breath is a way to calm yourself. You'll say to a friend, "Hey, chill. Take a deep breath." Take a deep inhale, and fill up the rib cage. Make a sound on the exhale.

Excellent. Let's do that again. I want you to scan for how that feels differently taking a deep breath than it did when you had your day-breath on. Just scan—notice if you feel differently in your shoulders, your chest. Notice whether you observe any difference. Now, put your hands on your rib cage and notice the deep breath filling up the ribs, and let it go again.

Now move your hands down to your belly, and fill it up with air. Does that actually lit-

erally happen? Not really, because obviously the air only goes into your rib cage. In yoga, it's called belly breathing. What I envision to help me with this is, I imagine the air going down my spine, which of course it doesn't really do, but I think of it going down my spine to my tailbone, and puffing out my belly when it arrives. Then my belly collapses as the breath goes back up the spine and out the nose, or the mouth. Practice bringing the air all the way down into your belly, puff the belly out, and exhale. Great.

All right, let's do that again. Into the belly—just feel your belly. Most people are not too fond of their bellies. We think our bellies are too flabby, or we don't have abs, or we just really try to suck it in. You see somebody cute, you try to hold in your belly. But actually, a really relaxed person has a relaxed belly. Just breathe in, and notice that your belly is sitting on a seat. Feel where you're touching the seat. Feel your legs coming down to the ground. Notice that you're rooted here safely in this moment. Bring your breath all the way down again. Not only are you going to bring the breath down to your tailbone, you're going to bring it down to the genitals. Some people have never breathed into their genitals before. They're not really getting a whole lot of air.

I want you to take your mind's eye and drop it down inside your belly and take a look around.

Look from the inside where you're sitting against the chair. Look at your belly that you maybe don't like too much. Look at your belly button. Look at your genitals from the inside. Just look around privately in your own sacred space. This is a beautiful place to make love from—with your awareness inside your own sacred space.

Bring the awareness up a bit to the navel, on the inside. Bring it up to the solar plexus, which is right below where the ribs come together in the middle. It's your power center. Breathe in there. Take a look around inside your lungs—inside.

Come to your heart, and notice if your heart is broken. Everyone you know has had their heart broken, every single one. Feel the state of your heart. Is it still broken? Is it healing? Is there a wall around it? Breathe air into it, a deep breath. Feel the vulnerability in your heart. A lot of people are afraid to love again, and maybe that's you. Notice that when you breathe, is the air bypassing the heart or going through it? A lot of people breathe in a pattern that goes around the heart rather than through the heart. It's self-protection. Who can blame them?

Bring your mind's eye up to inside your throat, and look at all the things you've been afraid to say in your life that have not passed through this barrier. All the times you wanted to tell someone you loved them; all the times you wanted to say something and just be heard; all the times you wanted to stand up and be strong and you just weren't able to yet. Notice if there's a barrier, for most people, probably for everyone; there's a strong barrier there at the throat of all the things that have not been said. All the things that weren't welcome—in the family you grew up in, in school, at your job, with your lover—all those words, thoughts, feelings, vulnerabilities were not welcome, so they stuck here in the throat. Look around inside.

Look at the layer of skin that surrounds your insides and feel where that barrier of skin touches the outside air. That's all that separates you from everything outside. Feel your skin. It's such a thin membrane.

Now notice that if you've been able to breathe and be in your body, the mind is blessedly silent. Osho used to talk about walking around as though we had our heads cut off—like headless people. It's a beautiful thing to be in silence inside our bodies and not have to think. Some people would call this meditation. You can live embodied like this. It can be your own secret. You could be sitting in a board meeting and nobody has to know that you're just enjoying being inside your own self, breathing, feeling what it's like against the chair, feeling the exquisite pleasure of the air going in and out of your nostrils. You can get high from just that if you really notice. It can be orgasmic to just sit and breathe. But whoever tells us that? This beautiful state can be practiced and cultivated. In tantra we try to remember this more. We try more and more to remember, "I am also my body."

The body is like a little dog that's so happy to be alive. There was a great meme on Facebook—I don't know if you saw it. It had a guy and his dog. The guy had his calen-

dar that had all the things he had to do. The dog also had a calendar, and it said "July 11th—This is the best day of my life." "July 12th—This is the best day of my life." "July 13th—This is the best day of my life." When you center in without thinking, "This is the best day of my life"—but the mind will tell you it's not.

When you're ready, come back and open your eyes, knowing that you can come back here at any time. If you choose to take this on as a practice, it will deepen and enrich your life. This is what is meant by being holistic; this is being both body and mind. Come back to the room, and bring your body with you. Welcome back.

About the Author

Catherine Auman, LMFT (Licensed Marriage and Family Therapist) is a spiritual psychotherapist and the Director of The Transpersonal Center. She has advanced training in traditional psychology as well as the wisdom traditions. Catherine lived for a year at the Osho ashram in India—a full-time immersion in tantra and meditation—and she has studied and practiced tantra, love, sex, intimacy, and seduction with numerous teachers. She lives in Los Angeles with her husband, Greg Lawrence, with whom she teaches tantra and relationship enhancement.

Connect with Catherine Auman

Websites   catherineauman.com

thetranspersonalcenter.com

Facebook   facebook.com/catherineauman.author

Instagram   @catherineauman

YouTube   youtube.com/@catherineauman

Create the Sex, Love, and Romance of Your Dreams with *The Tantric Mastery Series*

Imagine yourself in a perfect soulmate relationship full of sex, love and romance. Open yourself to love and awareness. These three beautiful books teach you how.

Catherine Auman's *Tantric Dating: Bringing Love and Awareness to the Dating Process* was named one of the **Best Dating Books of All Time by BookAuthority**. *Tantric Mating: Using Tantric Secrets to Create a Relationship Full of Sex, Love and Romance* follow up this success by teaching what to do next after attracting your perfect love to maintain the magic. *Tantric Relating: Relationship Advice to Find and Keep Sex, Love and Romance* is about how to communicate both verbally and non- to keep the love fires burning.

Buy Now online or at your favorite retailer

Print, eBook, or Audiobook

Scan the QR code below to purchase all of Catherine Auman's books on Amazon

Works by Catherine Auman

Books

The Tantric Mastery Collection: The Complete Tantric Mastery Series 3-in-1 Compilation

The Tantric Mastery Series (last three also available in Spanish)

> *Tantric Loving: Sacred Sexuality for Singles and Couples*
>
> *Tantric Relating: Relationship Advice to Find and Keep Sex, Love and Romance*
>
> *Tantric Mating: Using Tantric Secrets to Create a Relationship Full of Sex, Love, and Romance*
>
> *Tantric Dating: Bringing Love and Awareness to the Dating Process*

blissbody: Adventures in Tantra

Mindful Dating: Bringing Loving Kindness to the Dating Process

Guide to Spiritual L.A.: The Irreverent, the Awake, and the True

Shortcuts to Mindfulness: 100 Ways to Personal and Spiritual Growth

Fill Your Practice with Managed Care

Workshops

Tantra: The Science of Creating Your Soulmate

Tantra: The Foundations of Conscious Touch

Tantric Secrets about Women

Tantric Secrets about Men

Tantra and the Psychedelics of Sex

MDMA and Couples: The Promise of Ecstasy

Audio Recordings

Tantric Embodiment Induction

Deeply Relaxed

Awareness Breathing

www.ingramcontent.com/pod-product-compliance
Lightning Source LLC
Chambersburg PA
CBHW070241090526
44586CB00035B/1370